MW01041575

The Totally Awesome Joke Book for Kids

150 Ridiculously Funny Riddles for Kids of All Ages

BONNIE DALY

ISBN-13:
978-1543039528

ISBN-10:
1543039529

FOR CUFFY

The Totally Awesome Joke Book for Kids

❖ What do wizards write with?

Magic markers

❖ How do you get a rabbit to stay put?

Use hare spray

❖ Why didn't the tree get the joke?

It was stumped

❖ What happens when lightning hits the hen pen?

Fried chicken

❖ Why couldn't the mummy make any friends?

He was too wrapped up in himself

❖ How can you make a cow fly?

Use a cattlepult

❖ How can you keep a snow fort from caving in?

Use igglue

❖ What's better than chicken soup?

Chicken super

❖ What do you call a tasty pickle?

Dillicious

❖ What do garbage men eat?

Junk food

❖ Why do baseball players leave their cars at the stadium?

They like to run home

❖ What's the best month to hold a parade?

March

❖ What's green and splats on the wall at top speed?

Super Booger

❖ What kind of lizard tells funny jokes?

The sillymander

❖ What type of train has a dining car?

A chew-chew

❖ Why was the scab so sad?

He was getting picked on

❖ What do you call a shark that's a picky eater?

Finicky

❖ Who should you never throw a housewarming party for?

An Eskimo

❖ What did the cop say when he tried to arrest Jack Frost?

"Freeze!"

❖ How did the boy learn to play the violin?

He fiddled around with it

❖ How do you work the drawbridge on a castle?

Mote control

❖ What did the bird do when he forgot his speech?

He winged it

❖ Where do crabs buy their bread?

At crust stations

❖ What do soccer players wear in the rain?

Goalashes

❖ What kind of magic do witches use to help them concentrate?

Focus Pocus

❖ What type of primate never goes barefoot?

A sock monkey

❖ How do plumbers feel after a long, hard day at work?

Drained

❖ Where does winter footwear go on vacation?

Boot camp

❖ How did the mashed potatoes cross the river?

They rode in the gravy boat

❖ Why were the ghosts so sick?

They had the boo-bonic plague

❖ What do runners like to eat?

Fast food

❖ Where do lazy daisies hang out?

In flower beds

❖ What was the stable boy's name?

Barney

❖ What's black and white and red all over?

A zebra with a sunburn

❖ What type of shoes do plumbers hate?

Clogs

❖ What kind of meat it painful?

Cold cuts

❖ Why was the racecar driver's tongue so dirty?

He lapped his opponents cars

❖ What do you call an old goose?

A geezer

❖ What do you call a cat who eats lemons?

A sour puss

❖ What do you get when you eat too much Mexican Food?

A taco belly

❖ What happened to the van when it got broken into?

It was vandalized

❖ Why did the painting go to jail?

It was framed

❖ Where do snakes go skiing?

Aspen

❖ What's it called when stick figures get down?

Line dancing

❖ What do you call a fat Christmas tree?

A porky pine

❖ What type of art do Eskimos collect?

Ice sculptures

❖ What game do horses play at picnics?

People shoes

❖ How do bees groom themselves?

They use honey combs

❖ What do baby cows get when they eat too much candy?

Calf-ities

❖ What kind of lizard spends too much time online?

A computer monitor

❖ What's it called when a party beverage goes up your nostrils?

A punch in the nose

❖ How do creatures from the underworld like their toast?

On the dark side

❖ Who's the most likely knight to concede in battle?

Sir Ender

❖ Why did the monkey want the banana?

It had a peel

❖ What kind of food is good to eat at the beach?

Sandwiches

❖ How can you tell if a candy cane is new?

It'll be in mint condition

❖ Which Indian spread the most cold germs?

Chief Running Nose

❖ What do hogs use to write with?

Pig pens

❖ Why did the comedian tell so many bakery jokes?

He was on a roll

❖ Why didn't anyone like the snowman?

He was flakey

❖ What sucks about space?

Black Holes

❖ How did the ocean grab the attention of the lifeguard?

It waved

❖ What type of dinosaur always had a runny nose?

A Sinusaurus

❖ Why was the baker so rich?

He made a lot of dough

❖ Why didn't the turkey want any pie?

He was stuffed

❖ What insect is good with numbers?

The account ant

❖ How did the plumber know he was getting sick?

He felt flushed

❖ What do you call a frog from the wrong side of the pond?

Pond scum

❖ What's it called when you forget you ate strange meat?

Spamnesia

❖ What do you call a trailer in a tornado?

A mobile home

❖ Which foods give you great rhythm?

Drumsticks and beets

❖ What's the name of the gingerbread man's ship?

The Cookie Cutter

❖ What does a stove wear when it gets cold?

Oven Mitts

❖ How do old people get their false teeth to stay in place?

They use toothpaste

❖ Where do hogs stash their cash?

In piggy banks

❖ What are dinosaur jokes called?

Jurassic snark

❖ Where do baby cows go to cry over spilt milk?

The calf-a-tear-ia

❖ What type of pan should you never use to cook with?

A bed pan

❖ What movies does Mother Hen allow her babies to watch?

Chick flicks

❖ What did the dentist name his canine?

Fang

❖ Where can you pray for relief of dry skin?

In the chapel

❖ What happened to the actor who broke his leg?

The cast supported him

❖ What do prisoners use to make calls?

Cell phones

❖ What do you get when you mix a really big animal from Africa with a really big animal from North America?

A hippopotomoose

❖ Where do chess players buy stuff?

Pawn shops

❖ What happens when electricians get mad?

They blow their fuses

❖ What do you call a tire manufacturing plant?

A tread mill

❖ How did the student feel when his teacher changed his grade from a C to a D?

D-graded

❖ Why was the pencil sad when it's lead got broken?

It felt pointless

❖ What do you call ocean life that isn't blind?

See creatures

❖ What do you have when you live next door to a horse farm?

Nayyyyy-bors

❖ What do you call a crazy duck?

A loonatic

❖ What do you call a cave for baby bears?

A cubby hole

❖ What do doctors get when they study colds?

An achoo-cation

❖ Why was the hen mad?

The farmer was egging her on

❖ How do young bears learn wilderness skills?

They join the cub scouts

❖ What happens when a cow gets hit by lightning?

Instant hamburger

❖ What was the snakes favorite subject in school?

Hissssstory

❖ How can you tell when a snake is mad?

It throws a hissy fit.

❖ Why was the sponge so good at school?

He was good at soaking up information

❖ What was the name of the famous singing bird?

Talon Ted

❖ Why do porcupines have quills?

They hate writing in pencil

❖ What did the mouse say when he got his picture taken?

Cheese

❖ Why do dogs chase their tails?

They get in trouble when they chase the mailman

❖ How did the corpse get out of his coffin?

  It used a skeleton key

❖ What's short, green, and sheds?

  A leper-chaun

❖ Where do famous limes hang out?

  In the limelight

❖ What's it called when you chit chat with a clock?

  Tick talk

❖ Where do baby ghosts sit?

  In booster seats

❖ What do you call a dinosaur on a pogo stick?

A Bounce-a-saurus

❖ What insect can raise itself from the dead?

A zombee

❖ What two words can best describe both a good vacuum cleaner and a bad vacuum cleaner?

It sucks

❖ What's another name for a couch potato?

A dud spud

❖ What do you call a hog wearing a toupee?

A piggly wiggly

❖ Who's the celebrated leader of the lice?

Fabulouse

❖ Who do you call to fix a pier?

A dock-tor

❖ What do bunnies use in battle?

Pellet guns

❖ What do dentists do on their way to the bank?

Smile

❖ What do you call a stupid sweater?

A knit wit

❖ What did the Indian name his pet bird?

Tommy Hawk

❖ What was the title of the famous chicken farmer's biography?

Lord of the Wings

❖ What do you call it when a cow has diarrhea?

Chocolate milk

❖ What's it called when you go skydiving at no charge?

A free fall

❖ What kind of stories do hog farmers like?

Pig tales

❖ What do bad baseball players and judges have in common?

They both sit on the bench

❖ What medication do thieves take?

Klepto-bismol

❖ What types of illnesses are ducks prone to?

Mallardies

❖ What kind of doctor is good at poker?

A cardiologist

❖ What do ghosts play on the piano?

Sheet music

❖ When do tidal waves come up on land?

When they have shore leave

❖ What was the platypus after it got run over by a bus?

A flatypus

❖ What was Lassie's favorite vegetable?

Cauliflower

❖ What happened when the pig cooked a side dish?

Pork fried rice

❖ What happens when paint gets mad?

It fumes

❖ Why do birds fly?

They have frequent flyer miles

❖ What type of hair do mermaids have?

Wavy

❖ What do old ladies like to read?

Hagazines

❖ Why was the frog so still?

It was dead

❖ What do cannibals eat for lunch?

Manwiches

❖ What do you call it when you have no clue the guy sitting next to you is wearing a toupee?

Wignorance

❖ What do corpses do to pass the time?

Cryptograms

❖ What do you call a coyote who has a fit over everything?

A cryote

❖ What did the stick figure say when he robbed the bank?

"This is a stick up!"

❖ What do feisty rats have?

Rattitude

❖ What does King Kong use for a port-a-potty?

A dumpster

❖ Where did the farmer get his cows from?

A cattlelogue

❖ Where do they put insane dentists?

In dental institutions

ABOUT THE AUTHOR

Bonnie Daly lives in New London, Connecticut with her husband Tim and their son Cameron. When she's not busy trying to keep the two of them out of mischief she enjoys spoiling her pets, reading, playing the piano, tennis, camping, and writing humor—which is pretty much the only thing keeping her out of an asylum.

Visit her on the web at:
http://www.authorbonniedaly.com/

OTHER BOOKS BY BONNIE DALY

Surviving Gretchen, The Storms of Friendship Series, Book 1

Christmas Madness, Mayhem, & Mall Santas: Humorous Insights into the Holiday Season

The Totally Lame Joke Book

The Totally Disturbing Christmas Joke Book

Prescription for Laughter

Made in the USA
Columbia, SC
08 November 2017